SHINE, DARLING

Shine, Darling

ELLA FREARS

First published in 2020
by Offord Road Books

offordroadbooks.co.uk
@OffordRoadBooks

Typeset by Offord Road Books
Printed and bound in Great Britain by TJ Books Limited, Padstow, Cornwall

ISBN 978-1-916-01592-0

9 10

O•R•B

For J. T.

The hottest one for years of night

Contents

SHINE, DARLING

I Knew Which Direction

from the way the moon tilted towards the sea.
My heart, pulled gently from my chest, was carried,
   sleepwalking
over the waves. I held my breath, concentrated
on the new space. There was pain, but it was not new pain.

Pray now, whispered the sand and I fell to my knees thinking:
moonlight, moonlight, moonlight ————
until it was no longer a word but a colour and then a feeling
and then the thing itself.

Coming Into Your Own

there's something odd
              about pushing into yourself
the shape of that room
the furniture   when touched
            makes you forget where you are
a room that widens
and tightens at any sign of entry
            how you long for these
deaf dumb visitors   their careful rhythms
while above
            something wet slips off a kerb

The Overwhelming Urge

Stabbed in the arm with a compass.
      Stabbed in the side. Ink
                everywhere. Ink in her mouth.
Saint Sebastian of St Ives, holy
        on the supermarket roof
      throwing moss at passersby.

She's seen *Some Like it Hot* maybe twenty times.
        A hard kernel of a soul,
she practises softness.
      Pouted baby-mouth in the mirror:
              I used to sell kisses for the milk fund!

Stormy, sticky with flies,
        nettles brushing her ankles,
she bends,
      picks a dock leaf, rubs
        until the anklebone is green.

      A herd of cows gather to watch.

He wants to show her something
      by the metal farm gate.
She, nodding, surveys it from a distance,
      files it under:
             penis; moonlit.

      In the dark, the shapes of cows.

The ground is dirty with dirt. The air, dirty
with smoke; she, clean as a whistle, hops over the stile.
I used to sell kisses for the milk fund!

Below is the town, crammed in
against the yellow beaches
        and all around the sea is endless, aching.

While she wrestled him on the hill,
                the badgers, the horses, the sheep
worked away, shovelling
        their hearts into the landscape.

When he cried, the wind whisked his tears away
        and out to sea.   .

She has the overwhelming urge to jam
                her tongue into a plug socket,
        swing an axe
at her legs, swim out, out, out,
                        she's itchy with it.

For now there's nothing to do
                but finger one another
uncomfortably at the shoreline.

For now there's nothing
                to do but walk
together in the brilliant air, pick up lumps
                        from a freshly tilled field
        and ask – *rock or mud?*

The Film

The sun was shining as we
ambled around campus
stopping boys and men
and asking them to hit me
across the face.

They all refused
at first, but we explained
it was art and necessary
so they slapped me, one
after another.

I realised I had to
harden my eyes, provoke.
Each boy did a comedy slap – palm
to face, apologised before
and after. It was hot and bright.

We flirted with a geographer
whose slap was light, his fingers
just brushing my cheek as though
turning my face to the side to see
my profile. We had about

twenty guys on film.
My friend's boyfriend turned up
and we asked if he would do it.
He kissed her and stood to face me.
My friend pressed record, and said

'go' and I was laughing,
had forgotten to settle my face,
my left cheek slightly pink from
a day of slapping. I was not ready
for his backhand. Quick

and strong, a strange noise
as though he'd knocked the laugh
right off me, a thicker pain
than a sting, an immediate loss
of breath. For a moment,

we were silent, and I looked
at my friend whose hand had
flown to her cheek,
the camera's red light still
blinking and I knew

we would never watch
the film, that I would feel sick
and guilty as long as the bruise
lasted – longer – having asked
for what wasn't mine.

The (Little) Death of the Author

How many times, aged thirteen or so, did you send a text
saying *I'm in the bath . . .*
in reply to a boy you liked
asking you what you were up to?
And how many boys made you blush,
rosy and excited, by replying . . . *Can I join you?*

A triumph. You had succeeded, you
had made them think of you naked – the text
simple, factual. The image of your body's hot-water blush
suddenly the only thing they could focus on; the bath
or the idea of the bath *incredibly* steamy, allowing them to
say what they would like

to do, or at least, what they wanted you to think they'd like.
You were never in the bath, you
were always having dinner or trying to
finish homework. Text
and context are two different things. The bath
was a vessel into which you placed *the idea* of your blushing

body, (sent it across; innocent). His excitement, his blush
was on him. He didn't have to reply if he didn't like.
How clever you were! That ellipsis after *bath . . .*
an invitation to fill the gap . . . you . . .
All, of course, existing solely within the text.
There was no way for him to

come over, it was nine p.m. – too
late to have friends round – let alone boys (you blush
at the thought). No – any act was purely subtext.
When he asked to join you, he was asking if you liked
him: he sees your nakedness and raises you
lowering himself into the metaphorical bath.

In your mind it was a luxurious roll-top bath
no doubt. And to him your body was closer to
the women in films than a child's body. And you
had superimposed the penis you saw on a bus once, blushing
at the thought of *it* on him. Or maybe it wasn't like
that. Maybe the important part was the nakedness of the text,

which is a text I continue to send: *Reader, I'm in the bath . . .*
Nothing more to say than that. And if you like
you can join me. I'm blushing, are you?

Magical Thinking (1)

*To be without Tampax was to insure bleeding, to sleep naked
between white sheets was to guarantee staining.* — JOAN DIDION

We heard stories of girls scrubbing
with a toothbrush at first light,

of men vomiting, making them leave
and take the sheets with them.

The impulse on waking, to check
with fingers coming up clear each time –

a looseness imagined. Lily said
those girls hadn't listened to themselves.

We would. We knew to watch our tempers
and count the days. Fires were made,

stained garments were burned
along with the tips of our fingers

if we slipped up. *Control*
was Lily's favourite word. She knew

when it was safe, went out with nothing
on under her skirt – tempting fate.

We wouldn't shave if we wanted
to abstain that night – didn't work.

We had glorious full-bodied sex,
learned the boiling point of shame.

The hand is quicker than the eye, said Lily,
showing us how to slip a tampon out

and a man in with one swift movement.
How strong we felt, how filthy,

rolling on pale boys, brimming
with colour. We never forgot to tuck

the string up, to walk around naked
as though – nothing.

Magical Thinking (II)

Two adults in a taxi, a little drunk,
heading home from a family dinner.
One is my mother, the other, me.

Blushing, she tells me she 'came on'
unexpectedly during the party and bled
onto her aunt's favourite cushion.

What did you do? I ask.
I stole the cushion. She says.

She brings it out of her bag.
I look at it, my mother's stain – red-
brown, the ultimate Rorschach test.

The taxi swings round a corner and she grips
the little handle above the window.
Did Granny seem OK to you? she asks.

A storm cloud. A brain. That's what I saw.

Hayle Services (grease impregnated)

His head in the front seat
is parboiled. I'm feeling
pretty empty packet, salty
foil. *No point in worrying
until we know* but oh hello
turmoil. Boots. Up-down
the aisles *do you have an oily
complexion?* Woman at the till
tries to get my eyes with hers.
Avoid! Toilet-bound, *do you
have an oily . . .* M&S escalator
groans, shudders, fan belt
of the universe turning.
Can't go! Foiled again, but then
OK anxious stream. Feel grimy,
a bit doomy. Pissy hands.
Whisper: et tu uterus? Replay –
recoil. The overwhelming
sense that I'm on trial, soiled,
ruined, spoiled. Mamma,
can you come pick me up?
30 seconds. Still wet and blank.
I'm in Hayle, oh not much really,
just waiting for the pink voila.

Moon Myth

Because we donated our jewellery for the tabernacle
(by *we* I mean women and by *women* I mean allegories)
we have been assigned the moon.

Not *a* moon, *our* moon, our small, argumentative moon.
Sea of crisis and all – the old 'heave-ho stone' dragging
waves over pebbles since the dawn of time.

*58% of women say 'take what you're given, lest they assign us
an even smaller celestial body.'*

Everyone knows the fallopian tube is a moon-chute.

Everyone knows the sun is a boy-star, good and hot and
bright and pretty straightforward if you remember to pack
suncream. Of *course* it has a dick.

When I put a torch in my mouth my cheeks light up red
like a fleshy lantern – no silver, no waxing
or waning; I'm on or I'm off. Not very moon-like.

O Satellite, O Artemis, O Orb of the night.
Question: can I blame my lack of sleep on the moon?

*73% of women marked themselves 'uncomfortable' with the
new moon ritual we trialled last week, involving a pomegranate,
a starfruit (and some pretty heavy-handed apple symbolism).*

Time for another focus group. Maybe we can
burn stuff, or is fire a sun-only thing?

They poured some new wine into an old jug
and told us this is how myths are made.

We drank all the wine and exposed ourselves under
a full moon, so they must have been right.

Fucking in Cornwall

The rain is thick and there's half a rainbow
over the damp beach; just put your hand up my top.

I've walked around that local museum a hundred times
and I've decided that the tiny, stuffed dog,
labelled *the smallest dog in the world*, is a fake.

Kiss me in a pasty shop with all the ovens on.

I've held a warm, new egg on a farm and thought about fucking.
I've held a tiny green crab in the palm of my hand.

I've pulled my sleeve over my fingers and picked a nettle
and held it to a boy's throat like a sword.

Unlace my shoes in that alley and lift me gently onto the bins.

The bright morning sun is coming and coming
and the holiday children have their yellow buckets ready.

Do you remember what it felt like to dig a hole all day
with a plastic spade just to watch it fill with sea?

I want it like that – like water feeling its way over
an edge. Like two bright-red anemones in a rock pool,
tentacles waving ecstatically.

Like the gorse has caught fire across the moors and you
are the ghost of a fisherman who always hated land.

Visitation

I lie across the pond then play dead at the bottom of your glass.
  I turn up the heating and all the flies wake up.
    It's a long way to the next warm month.

This may not look hard just hanging around
    but the pressure builds and I feel heartbroken daily,
  have to pick things up and hurl them.

Please understand it's not *at* you it's *with* you.

I am a huge sail billowing dramatically in a light breeze.
    If I could just taste the air, if I could even just press
  my face against the window and feel the cold on my cheek.

I open my mouth like a dog and pant in your ear.

The red brick against the thin pale blue sky is no comfort.
  I can see an insect on the window pane, green and translucent.
I can see the dark shape of its organs working as it crawls.

It's nearly night now, I'm not even joking.

Bad news settles on my chest like a cold each morning.
    I climb inside your jumper, stay cocooned
  until you become hot and itchy, cast us both aside.

I try to touch the running water from the tap.

I make myself very big and stride across the fields.
    I'm careful not to look, no, not even glance
  at the small patch of grass where it happened.

The Flamingo Estate

The sun is setting and the house's eyes are burning gold.
Red hot pokers, ebullient and upright, line the stone steps
like torches. Just outside the door, someone's cigarette
smokes itself on the ground.

With the blind pulled down, the air in the room
is the colour of rye – like fucking in a basket.
She thinks of the bath she'll run later,
a different kind of nakedness. She thinks

of steam – a natural soft focus. There's a place
down the road that sells cakes impossibly heavy
with cream. There's a palm tree nearby so enthusiastic the sky
has had to make extra room.

She shuts her eyes so that they can see her better,
becomes aware of her own mouth. Meanwhile, a river
splits in two, stretches its lovely long legs towards the sea.

Joan of Arc is Haunting Us

She knows how glass shivers before the rock is thrown,
how pipes hiss like snakes at one another
through the house. She's felt a mushroom's first push

upwards, has mapped her shadow's sly progress
across the changing ground. She listens
for the tiny thud of a rabbit's heart; she's always loved

the warmth of blood even as it leaves the body, sinks
into the mud. She's felt the quick slap of a gunshot,
the slow sweep of a deer's tongue, she knows that pain

forms in the mind like frost. The sun bakes her body,
her ears cupping small pools of shade in the blaze,
the sound of a plane above hums through her.

On bad days she ties her clothes in complicated
knots, encourages passersby to do the same.
Hush, Joan, we say. *Why don't you count the croci.*

Existential

Sandwich,
verge,
you come to realise
that you
are surrounded
by rats.

Verge, sandwich,
you come to realise
that you
are a rat.

WELCOME
says the sign
WELCOME
BREAK. Your nose
twitches wetly
in a puddle
of milkshake.

A blackbird nearby
eyes you like a
hot dinner.
What then?
You whisper.

Crisps fall
about you
like rain
through the
slats of a
picnic table.

Phases of the Moon / Things I Have Done

New Moon: I ransacked the house for something that does not exist.
Waxing Crescent: I ate twelve peaches.

First Quarter: I Tipp-Exed an old letter from him, leaving only the word *basement*.
Waxing Gibbous: I put on my favourite underwear and cried in the mirror.

Full Moon: I buried a pork-chop in the garden, walked backwards, howled.
Waning Gibbous: I thought a great deal about drilling a hole in my head.

Third Quarter: I told the neighbour my heart beats only for her.
Waning Crescent: I stood outside facing the house, waited for myself to appear.

Captivity is Justified

When I look into her tank she turns away from me,
says the scientist on the TV, *She's coy!*
Lab coat, shiny face, pipette trembling above a spider.

Oh that golden summer! A brace of ducks
at my heels wherever I went. Eels, fifty years old
snaking through the river towards our nets.

I'd say Augustus the llama was more of a childhood
acquaintance than a pet. Basil the (chestnut) bull – an idol.
A seal once tugged the zip of my wetsuit down . . .

While playing hide and seek as a child,
I interrupted my friend's old ginger cat
who had been licking a wall.

The room was unlit and shadowy. The cat, George,
had long limbs. I was the only human around.

George turned from the spot he'd been licking; yowled *die.*

Chicken in my oven, buttered. Goldfish in my fish-tank, bored.
All I want's a puppy, a little puppy to adore.

These are my lovers

what of it? Closer to dogs than men. Closer
to donkeys than dogs. Their old-fashioned skirts leave
everything to the imagination.

Picture this: week-old meat. Picture this:
buttered toast picked up off a dirty carpet.
I whistle and they come (Pavlov, eat your heart out).

I stroke their matted heads and they snore
at my feet, content.

If they misbehave I send them to bed
without any supper; they love supper – crouching
over their plastic bowls like harpies.

If they're good I let them count the freckles on my arms.

I'm not saying it's what I want forever. I'm saying
times are hard and gratitude really does it for me.

Tonight, I will enter their bedroom in nothing
but a heavy gold necklace. I will hold my arms out,
palms upwards and from their twin beds

they will rise, softly, like smoke from the altars of villages.

AND SAND AND SAND AND SAND

for W.

I have this friend who's into sand / not like the beach / sand
you might use in construction / the economics of sand / buy-
ing and selling sand / not that he buys or sells / but he enjoys
/ for example / that there is a black market for sand / this
friend is a writer / he writes novels in which the characters
are obsessed with sand / buried in sand / swallow some sand
stuck to a sandwich / when he describes the act of eating sand
/ he describes it so vividly / I know he's done it / I don't even
need to ask / he likes to eat things / he's a good cook / he
also ate a lover's hair / once / it's not like he's got a sand fetish
/ although / scrutinise anything long enough / it might as
well be your kink / there's porn for everyone now / I'm sure
there's sand porn / I google sand porn / an hour has passed
and it's just sand-coloured bodies / on a beach / and I don't
feel any different / and yet I am changed / walking through
the city / with this friend who used to love cities / but now
loves sand / I wonder if there is anything left / to be interest-
ed in / get off my sand / he'll say when he reads this / but this
isn't about sand / it's about those times / I've fallen asleep at
parties / and woken to him / high as the great dune of Pilat
/ his eyes like gaping coal pits / which doesn't fit the theme
/ but boy are those eyes black / kneeling over me /saying /
don't sleep / don't sleep yet / and although the sofa is deep /
and my limbs are deadweights in the shallow end of the pool
/ I do get up / and I'm glad to watch us / two misshapen
grains / buffeted / angular / dancing as the sun cuts across the
window / in a building / twenty miles wide / twenty miles
high / stretching further than our tiny human eyes can see

Becoming Moss

I lie on the ground.
I open my mouth.
I suck on a spoon.
I embrace a stone.
A beetle crawls by.
I empty my mind
I stuff it with grass
I'm green, I repeat.

The sun is a drink
the yellowest squash
I can't get enough
I can't get enough
I can't get enough
I can't get enough
I can't get enough
I can't get enough

Darling, a dream is not the place to tell me that you're leaving

You knew I wouldn't be able to return, having staged the break-up
in the manor house I revisit most nights but cannot name.
Each time a new interior and in every room I feel hungry and eat a lot.

My heartbeat thickened to a sob, velvet rubbed the wrong way.
I hit out at the air, which was woolly, saturated with the sound of running water.

I'm going, you whispered. And I saw your lips moving over the threshold,
felt my dry cough of a question I was already answering.

I pulled a shroud of souls across my body which might have been the duvet.

I looked at the empty doorway which was now an enormous archway.
I'll get a gun, I thought. I'm pregnant, I thought. I'm hungry, I thought.

Everybody Has to Wee

1

I learned to wee alone in a damp bungalow
surrounded by fields and magic stones.

I called it a 'vee vee'. A party was thrown in my honour.
By the stream, I stung my bottom on a nettle.
The pagans wept.

In the house I saw pictures in the peeling wallpaper –
a man in an enormous hat, a tornado, a whale;

foresaw my death. Made a puddle on the carpet.

2

Once, drunk, in the middle of the road,

I aimed the stream downhill and through
my friend's legs – a nutmegging.

3

In an Irish peat bog, I woke in a tent
full of sleeping bodies, desperate.

It was a bright dawn, the air
tasted green and fertile.

I hiked to the top of a small hill. And there,
with no one around, the whole lush landscape
at my feet, I lifted my skirt and squatted.

Just then – a low-flying helicopter
with a film crew inside

so close I could see their faces.

4

More than once, crouching behind a bush, I've accidentally
pissed on an ants' nest. Of course I apologised, swerved,
splashed my shoes, but also felt acutely
how forceful I can be.

How many humans in the history of humans
have been made to feel like God by a swarm of ants?

I felt so empowered I marched right out of that wood
and got the man and got the job and bought the car
I truly deserve.

5

Those times that you're also in the bathroom
brushing your teeth
and I sit sort of side-saddle to look cute.

6

Only a little bit in a deep brown river
when a large fish swam towards me.

7

The first normal wee after a bout of cystitis!

Immortalise that moment in marble
and you'd have something close to the ecstasy
of Saint Teresa.

8

You and I exit our separately gendered toilets
simultaneously, like a dance. We pass the tiny casino,
head to Costa without saying a word.

Lightness. Efficiency.

Ready to fill the new space.

9

In a mug. In a sink. In a little cup
to give to the doctor.

Walking Home One Night

I catch the moon winking through the trees.
I'm gripping my house-keys between my knuckles.
It's like glimpsing an old friend through a crowd.

I soften. She is a sliver, towards the soft end of yellow.
I breathe in the night, lift my fingertip to fill in the circle.
Turning onto the stretch of road that I don't like, lampless
    and narrow,

I tell her: *I will be calling on you, to testify*
that you saw the whole terrible thing through one half-closed eye.

Midpoint

I'm an inconsolable piglet
rooting for lumps in the snow.

                               Incrementally it falls.
A blanket of hours
       across the boarded-up restaurant.

                                  Daylight
has eased off but the neon green strip
               along the edge of the petrol station
       has picked up the slack.
I've never seen a colour try so hard.

                             Thoughts, like water,
take the route of least resistance.
                     Mine course up
       and down the motorway.
I shove
            a Scotch egg into my mouth.

                 Looking backwards
off the A30 – there I am,
                 swimming under the fat lip
of a cliff,
       refusing another lift from the maths teacher.

Further on,
            I'm aimless on the harbour front,
on the dunes.
       Throwing punches

in a novelty captain's hat.
Sharing a cigar with the boy
my best friend likes.

In the toilets,
I'm in the mirror.
Sobbing over a row of sinks.
The soap dispensers dribble
silky puddles
on the faux-marble counter.

The road ahead is dark.
Snowy banks on either side.
The ghosts of verges past.
Leaning against a pump,
I watch the red lights head onwards.

Would you mind, sir, hitting pause
on the CCTV, running it backwards
so that I might watch
the sky getting a taste
of its own cold medicine?

More than once
I've slowed, to take a long drink
of someone else's collision.
Madam, filling up your dusty Peugeot,
it's OK to stare. Come,
let me wipe my puffy eyes on your trouser leg.

PASSIVITY, ELECTRICITY, ACCLIVITY

For years after my near-abduction
I told my mother I could smell him, still

    that was easier than explaining

that it wasn't so much him I could smell,
but something new in me.

I heard a story about a man who made shoes for spies. These shoes were made to be given to the enemy. At first, they would feel perfectly comfortable, but over time they would change the enemy's gait, making them walk with a slight limp which would register in others as a lack of confidence. Their self-assurance would begin to wane and an ache would develop somewhere deep inside their bones; the enemy would sicken, would have to take leave from work. These shoes would inexplicably change the shape of their feet so that no other shoes felt right. The enemy would form an attachment which, over time, would become a compulsion; they would never go anywhere without the shoes, might even begin wearing them in bed. The enemy's partner would grow weary, would leave them for someone easier, less fraught. The enemy would drink for the pain, lose hope and wonder why the circulation in their toes was so bad that in the winter they were blueish-black. This condition would spread to their feet, then their legs, and because they were now the nervous type who would not want to

bother the doctor, it would all be left too late and they'd
lose something – a toe if they were lucky, a foot if not.

★

A boyfriend who thinks I have seen him kissing
another girl outside the rugby club tells me
he couldn't bear how heartbroken I looked;
how he regretted it the moment he saw
how much it mattered to me.

I hadn't seen.

I had been tasting the cold air,
feeling my heart   beat
into the dark car park,
the thrill of my presence
under the sky alone,

            or so I thought;

maybe there is always someone watching,
maybe there is always someone to tell you
that your heart has broken

        no matter how whole you feel
beside the bins
        and under the stars.

★

Things develop. We measure:

flour into a bowl, softness of an avocado,
my breasts which won't stop growing
       (the reminder of a possibility I refuse to measure),

I measure threat, which is a dull ache
 when I am out of the house
      and a freezing immersion at night.

★

There used to be a small theme-park where I grew up called 'Merlin's Magic Land', just out of town. On the roundabout in front, a man would stand dressed as a wizard, waving to all the cars and pointing at the theme-park. This man who was paid to dress as Merlin, began to think he *was* Merlin. He'd hang around town in his costume, just waving and pointing – in the supermarket, on the pier, through café windows. In the height of summer when all the tourists were out on the beach, pink and near-nude, Merlin would sit on the sand, his face pale under his hat. One day, he picked up a toddler and began to wade into the sea. Who knows what he was trying to do; drown it, baptise it? When the mother screamed he looked surprised to find a child in his arms. He didn't get far. Two years later the theme-park shut down. We never saw Merlin again. Maybe he died. Maybe he moved away. Maybe no one recognises him without the costume.

★

The night of my near abduction,
the hotel manager took me into the room
of a man who fitted my description.

We crept in and stood over his sleeping
body, together in the dark, *is it him?*
I strain to see, afraid of what will happen
if his eyelids lift. *No.*

★

My uncle is into healing. He has thin lips
and when a song plays about God he shuts his eyes
and reaches upwards.

I heard that the enemy wearing the shoes
will either find God or lose It.

★

At a party a boy follows me into the bathroom
claiming that when I left the room
I nodded for him to follow.

Did I?
Did he know that I hadn't?

I let him in, because
why not take what I'm told I want –
who knows, he might be right.

★

He calls to check
that I haven't given him a false number,
leaves me a voicemail with my nipple
in his mouth.

The next morning, alone, I listen to his voice –
a child talking with his mouth full

and then me,
like a dull, distant mother:

gently, gently, gently.

★

In the restaurant, on the roof terrace
you are facing me and I am watching the moon
rise against a bright blue sky behind you.

Baby, I want to say, *hold the moon a second
I'm already carrying so much.*

I order a steak, rare, and try to feel strong,
the blood coating my tongue as both you
and the moon intensify.

★

The evening after my near abduction, I am with my cousins
in a hotel room, playing cards. They know the rough details
and are excited and a little freaked out.

When no one is looking I hide behind the curtain,
wait for a few minutes, then knock softly on the window.
They scream and suddenly I am more afraid than I have
     ever been.

★

At school we used to say that if you said *Merlin*
five times while looking into a mirror
he would appear behind you.

I think about this every time I see my reflection.

★

I write a letter to the girl who was abducted
because I failed to identify a sleeping man.

Dear —,

I thought I was special, chosen.
I walked out of that room thinking he was my problem
to leave sleeping. Please understand.

★

I lived in a house for a year with six strangers.
One of them was a Catholic girl called Lucy.

Two weeks in, though we'd barely talked
she told the others in the house

42

that we'd slept together.

   It was a mistake, I feel sick she told them.

★

I overhear Lucy telling a friend how it happened.

There are the usual elements – *wine, secrets shared,
laughter, a light touch and then . . .* and then

   there are the odd specifics:

the way I kissed her *(too hard),*
   how I kept saying   *you're fun*

after each move towards undressing her.
It was so vivid, I nearly believed it.

★

The police arrive.

   We've been called by your neighbour.
Your housemate is hanging out of the fourth-floor window,
threatening to jump.

I go into the kitchen, Lucy is on the window ledge
barely holding on with two fingers.

   We are going to hell
            she shouts at me.

43

★

Dear —,

Do we look alike?
I have always wondered what would have happened
if I had gone with him.

What would have happened?

★

When I think back on Lucy,
I see myself doing the things she said I did.

★

I find a Dictaphone taped to the underside of my bed.
I ask Lucy if it's hers. *Yes,* she says,

I wanted to hear you sleep.

I have nothing to say. I hand the Dictaphone over
without deleting the recording.

What can a woman take from a woman?

★

I return home to see family. It's October 31st. There is a
small witch in fishnets at the train station. I take the bus
towards town. It's at that point just before dark when

the sky looks thin and yellow-pink and everything seems cinematic. I lean my face on the glass. My eye, reflected, is a part of the darkening road outside. I watch it clarify as the landscape fades. As we pause for the lights, I shift my focus through my face and then I see him, on the roundabout in front of what is now new flats – Merlin. Except his face is made-up like a skull. There is no one else around. He looks right into the bus and waves at me. An obscure joke, I think. A quiet one.

★

Lucy claims to have also had a Dictaphone
under the kitchen table, that she now knows
all the secrets in the house.

>   *The others are so awful about you*   she tells me.

And in spite of myself I ask what was said.

★

I can only assume Lucy has been feeding secrets
to everyone. We've all stopped talking, eat in our rooms,
pass one another silently in the hall.

Someone is pregnant says Lucy from my doorway
>   *Do you want to know who?*

>   I'm eating cereal on my bed.
>   I don't even look up.

When she's gone I send a text to the others:

Lucy is a liar.

The next morning,
my milk in the fridge has been dyed green.

★

At college I knew a girl called Millie,
she was a few years older, but we always
stopped to talk if we bumped into one another.

We had the same driving teacher – a large
Welsh man called Bill.

Bill was obviously in love with her.

One day, sitting in the college library,
I get a phone call.

This is Millie's dad, can you talk?

Yes.

[It takes me a second to place who she is]

I'm afraid Millie has passed away.

How? [the wrong question]

She took her own life, [silence]

[to himself] *she looked so peaceful.*

I'm sorry   I say [finally]

                      and he rings off.

★

On the bus home that afternoon I think of Millie;
the little I know about her. She is/was beautiful.
She has/had an identical twin who I met once.

I wonder what it's like to lose someone who shares
your face.
I wonder how Millie did it and why. *Pills* I think
must be the most peaceful.

I play back all those encounters
but can't find any signs. She always looked at ease.
Happy. Enviable.

She had texted only a couple of days ago
asking if I wanted to meet for a coffee and catch up.
I reread the text.

I ask myself how I feel, but can't reach anything sub-
stantial.

★

That evening I have a driving lesson.
Bill seems annoyed.

Millie was supposed to have the hour before yours
but she didn't bother turning up

47

with some boy no doubt.

I know I should say something but I don't.

That's the problem with beautiful girls, he says,
they think they can get away with murder.

Take the next left.

★

*I ignored the brilliant boy when he cut a skyline
across his stomach with a steak knife.*

*I ignored the thin girl when she ate raw chicken
straight from the fridge.*

*I told the woman who was afraid of her own thighs
that I didn't want to see them either.*

Who is this for? – me? you?
   I never drove again.

★

Working at a bar one night I notice
a handsome older man staring at me.

He apologises, tells me he has just separated
from his wife. *She moved out today.*

He says I look just like she did
when they met twenty years ago.

People push to be served, the music is loud,
I wait for his Guinness to settle.

There are large tears rolling down his face.
Nobody else has noticed.

Christ, you're so like her he whispers
as I hand him his change.

★

I ask myself if I'd ever give you the shoes.

    I decide, that in those moments
that I want to hurt you,
    it's a lightning bolt I'd like to send,
not an undertow.

★

He's waiting for me outside when I finish my shift.
I agree to go for a drink with him somewhere nearby.
He has nice eyes. He tells me about his wife, how they
    met.
He cries twice. The pub closes.

I live two minutes away, he says, *come for a drink, I can't be
    alone.*

At his house surrounded by his wife's possessions
he shares a joke with himself on my body.
Mostly, it seems to be some sort of reenactment,
but towards the end it feels more like a vendetta.

On my way to the bathroom I pause at a photo
of a couple on a beach, laughing. He looks so young,
tanned – embracing a beautiful woman
who looks nothing like me.

★

The man who made the shoes took his own life.

The day before, he sent a parcel to his son –
a pair of shoes, well-worn but beautiful,
no explanation.

The son threw them away. They weren't close.

★

Baby, hold the moon a second —

★

The moment the abduction became a *near* abduction
was a matter of balance.

There was me – a freckled ten year old
with boy-hair and a desire to be wanted.

There was him, asking again and again sweetly,
Ça va Ella?   *Ça va Ella?*   *Ça va Ella?*

★

There was the way, as we walked up the hotel stairs,
arm in arm, I shifted my hip so there was room
to break free and ran off slowly, laughing, as if
it were all a game.

That I knew to laugh like that aged ten surprises me.
That same laugh escapes my mouth almost every time
I leave the house   *I don't know,*   *I don't mind,*
I'm sorry   it says.

★

Then, the moment when I had the key
in the door and he realised I was going to get away
the balance tipped.

He stood still at the end of the corridor
and shouted, like a teacher, like an angry father,

Ella, Come here NOW

and I very nearly went.

★

The thing about telling you the story of my near-
abduction is that I have to put on his voice, say the things
he said – first sweetly then severe. I see the effect
on dinner party guests, on my parents, on you when I told
    you.
For a moment I am him. I have to become him – other-
    wise
it doesn't work; otherwise none of this works.

★

At a New Year's Eve party,
two years after her death, I see Millie.

It's not her, of course, but her twin.
She's dancing with her eyes shut, there's glitter on her face.

You were the last person she texted
she says, hugging me tightly,
        the first of her friends my dad called.

She is high and strokes my hair.
I'm so happy to see you, she says, laughing,
I miss her so much.

She looks into my eyes with Millie's face
and kisses me.

I say nothing, I open my mouth.
Who am I to say no to this?

The music is loud and when she pulls away
she is crying.

You're fun

I hear myself say.

You, a St Ives Modernist,

are trapped in a disastrous and destructive marriage with the War, so you begin an affair with the Atlantic Ocean . . . and a sailor, and a sculptor, and Paris, and New York, and a stone circle, and a Cornish hedgerow fizzing with cow-parsley. Nine months later you give birth to a white square and you're not sure who the father is.

Barbara Writes to the Reverend

a cento

alas, the blind organist is leaving
but you were the sun on Thursday
the sound of sea & wind & even birds
The reticulata, snowdrops, croci are out &
I got into deep water
I thought a lot about how much love surrounds us,
you, Frank & even me & it is all too easy to forget this,
thinking of the absent son
My problem is, always, what to confess,
beyond sloth, indulgence & selfishness
The agony of the wilderness
this hideous notepaper
Is my deep love for Ben, now married again for 11 years,
    a sin?
My lovely children whom I so love absolved me
I'm scarcely a parishioner though my spirit is so
I know there is not much time left to me
beset by ill health
confusion comes &
I hope so much to see this spring
forgive the muddled writing
You may be needed
how lovely it will be to see you
a great beautiful surprise & just full & full of music
I have realised that one must relinquish all,
in order to understand anything
My Bardic name is now GRAVYOR.
Rather nice?

Words taken from Barbara Hepworth's letters to Dean Donald Harris, 1969, Tate Archive

You, a Teenager,

at St Ives School just after the millennium are red-faced, insisting *IT. IS. ART. BECAUSE. THE ARTIST. SAYS. IT IS.* in response to your English teacher's dismissal of Tracey Emin's bed. You bat away every *so if I put a brick . . .* and *my two-year-old could've . . .* but you, a teenage girl, on a table of boys (in the hope that you'll be a good influence) don't yet have the linguistic skills to argue this point. The teacher tells you *enough now*, and you open *Of Mice and Men* and the boys ruffle your hair, chanting *don't muss it up, don't muss it up . . .* in a faux Southern–American drawl. And you think, Emin probably dealt with men and boys like these, Hepworth too, in her way. And you think, at least we're engaging. At least this book is good. You knew the art was art, and anyway – you quite liked it when they touched your hair.

Alfred / Wallis

(1942)

He dreams of his boat, tossed about like a flea
on a dog's back. At night the sea is lead-
coloured. The sea is always feral.

He can feel the devil's wet ear
pressed against his chest. When he wakes, fear
lights up his mind like a flare.

(2018)

I pass through the gate, past the low tree I
used to climb, the grass is springy, is
damp and I catch the salt air like a sail
as I face the sea for the first time. I'll
weave my way down, touch a tile – palm flat – a
superstition, a pilgrimage, something I saw
my mother do. She'd whisper, *thanks, Alfred Wallis*,
then wander into town. Stone path, stone walls . . .
I've left Barnoon. I've left St Ives. But all day I will
be thinking of perspective, of lighthouses as jaunty as
sailors, of what a sweet, raw talent he was.

You, a Section of Colour in a
Heron Painting,

hover just over the surface of another colour, so close
you might be brothers, though what does it matter now
that you're in opposition? Together you hum like an
electric eye.

The light you emit is deep and absorbent. You pos-
sess warmth. Not the heat of a lover or even the yellow
embrace of a parent, but the subtle warmth one might
feel while watching a film that's set in the Mediterranean.

You've tried to imagine being red, being burnt-out
and blunt; bright as a slap across the face. But you never
quite get there.

It's like picturing winter on a hot July day – no
matter how much snow you conjure, you won't feel cold.
There's a warm sea fog on the horizon and you'll always
be blue.

On Stringing the Form

They're the gust of sea-wind buffeting you
as you walk down the beach; the sexual ambiguity
of your friend's friend that you're hitting on in a bar.

   You're driving through a tunnel;
          you're holding your breath.

They're seven firm sentences broken
across an idea; a single thread of spider's web
strung across two sleeping bodies; the stitches
in your stomach-wound as you reach for the remote;

   a car teetering on a cliff-edge for sixty years.

They're the suspense as you wash your face, knowing
that the odds of a murderer being in your house
have increased while your eyes were shut;

   the fever-pitch this fear reaches as you
          close the mirrored bathroom cabinet.

They're not your sense of self, spread thinly
on your morning toast; they can't seduce
your mother in a hotel lobby. But they are
a paper airplane thrown across a smoky room,

   and they're exactly like waking
          to the eyes of an insomniac.

You're walking home from a meeting / a play /
the shops, carrying the ingredients for the dinner
you've decided to make – swinging the bag slightly
or just feeling the weight of what will be.

The evening is a soft blue / orange, the air
is not cold, not warm. Out of nowhere
you feel insignificant in the most luxurious way

and just at that moment the streetlamp
you're walking under switches on, like enlightenment.
There's no one around.
You just feel that feeling and carry on home.

Strings – threaded and fixed:

   an enormous feeling, contained within
           a small body, under an enormous sky.

You, a Poet Researching Naum Gabo,

accidentally request the original documents rather than the translations in the archive. You're distracted when the archivist hands you the box and she says something you don't quite hear. You nod and take the file. When you reach the desk you realise that she said, *These are in Russian.* You pretend to read them for thirty-five minutes.

Resistance

We slept under a full moon. Our bodies wound
like pale snakes through the silver-tipped grass.
We opened our mouths and let the light fall in.

Have you ever tried it? It's the closest light
to water, pooling on your eyelids, cool
and wordless on your tongue.

We slept deeply, eyes open. We felt the weight
of the water in the air and wild laughter
began to well up inside. We threw back
our spotlit heads, let it pour until morning.

Whenever you see a tall, glass building

you imagine it inside you.
The everyday burlesque: salting
a pan of water, bending
to pick up yesterday's clothes.

Walking through your garden
at night you pause at a rosebush,
kneel, feeling ancient. A monk
in a monastery garden. Pulling

a long stem towards you,
you take the whole petalled head
in your mouth. Dew-cold, velvet,
grassy-tasting. You let it rest

on the bed of your tongue. Over
the wall there are more gardens –
garden after garden squared-off
like stills in a reel of film.
The moon behind you

has its hand on the back of your head.
Mouth full you catch the eye
of a distant skyscraper,
wink.

Premonition

He wakes me up saying, *well . . . guess what's happened.*
A sad half-laugh, and I push the covers over my face.

Behind closed eyes there's a woman standing in a lake alone,
the bottom of her coat trailing in the water.

When I wake again he's gone to work. On my phone,
I scroll through headlines, reactions; my brother-in-law posts:

YES! Now let's line them up against a wall!

And I flood with rage, wishing I'd tried
to stem his *OUT OUT OUT.*

I open the message box, close it.

On my way to Greenwich Park, a man pulls over,
asks me to suck his cock and I stare blankly ahead;

couldn't tell you what he looked like.

I imagine my brother-in-law's jubilance and want to hurt
something, want to stop people in the street and apologise.

But where was I? My little badge shining like a beacon.

I reach the top.

A man in a Union-Jack hat is smoking against the
    observatory.
A family hops from one side of the meridian line to the
    other.

The air in the park smells fantastic.

As I walk back down I pass a small body of water
and wonder if my dream was a premonition.

A woman nearby on her phone shakes her head.
I mean, what the fuck? She says, *what the actual fuck?*

I wade in to self-fulfil.

ETA

Bastard
grey road.
Empty sky.
Radio – dull,
dull songs.
Even you,
who I love
fiercely, are
fucking me
off. On our
way to a party.
Family party.
Obligatory.
Last time
I saw Uncle
I shouted *you
are the patriarchy!*
Driving home
post summit
post pride–
swallow
I talked
and talked.
Exeter Services,
cried again.
You, tired,
told me
I was right.
Didn't help.

Box of bad
cocktail sausages,
Diet Coke.
Now, it's
Taunton Deane,
the present,
no
less tired.
Coffee smell.
The urge
to punch
a nice old
man, a child.
Cry
uselessly
at 60mph.
Watching
your eyes
watch
the road.
Indicator,
tick, tick, tick,
off.
T-minus ten.
In the flip-
down mirror.
Fixing
mascara,
my smile.

After the Lie, Donald came in a vision to Donald

On the twenty-
fourth day the river,
a belt of gold,

Donald like topaz,
like lightning, eyes
flaming, arms

burnished
leading himself
into the river.

I, Donald
touched my lips
and used lotions.

On the twenty-
fifth day the river,
a cord of honey,

Donald like flint,
like thunder, eyes
closed, arms

bare
chasing himself
into the river.

I, Donald
opened my mouth and sang
what I had rehearsed.

On the twenty-
sixth day the river,
a dark rope,

Donald like touch-paper,
like ice-storm, eyes
black, arms

bleeding
dragging himself
into the river.

I, Donald
vision of such terror
I fled.

On the twenty-
seventh day the river,
a dry trough,

Donald like sawdust,
like swarm, eyes
aching, arms

weeping
digs in the dirt
for the river.

I, Donald
touched my lips
but nothing came.

On the twenty-
eighth day the river,
a splitting headache,

Donald like salt,
like aftershock, eyes
restless, arms

frantic
tries to plug the source
of the river.

I, Donald
could not escape
my lips.

On the twenty-
ninth day the river,
an unmade bed,

Donald like piss,
like epidemic, eyes
raw, arms

heavy
buried himself
in the river.

I, Donald
swallowed the dust
until I drowned.

Elegy for the Cassini Spacecraft

1997–2017

I was thinking about your death. I was trying to imagine the moment when the pressure becomes too great or the heat too much.

And then at about four o'clock in the afternoon I heard awful screaming. Sound carries strangely in our cul-de-sac and I couldn't work out if it was in the distance or just under my window.

Part of the horror is not knowing what's making the sound. That's why in good films, the *bad thing* is only glimpsed or not seen at all. I stood in my doorway trying to work it out: a dog was barking, a man was shouting, a woman was screaming.

And then I heard a body being struck with an object. I knew it was a *body* and not a *thing* by the way the other sounds bent around it. The traffic, the screaming, the trees and the wind all warped by this blunt, irregular thumping. I ran towards it.

Behind a low fence, a man was beating a dog with a shovel. There were neighbours in windows and on the street, watching. There was the distant sound of sirens and the man stopped and went inside.

The dog was silent, looking blankly at the sky. We gathered round the fence. It was breathing, and then it wasn't.

Cassini, today, as you dived between Saturn's rings gathering data, I saw a dog die – a detached but very real sadness. A weary, inner *ohh*, like a small balloon deflating.

The other dogs in the cul-de-sac wouldn't stop barking until morning. They knew. I doubt it will be the same for you. I can't imagine crows rising suddenly from the trees, or an old woman on her way home inhaling sharply: *it's gone!*

Last night my dreams were full of that sound – shovel against dog. One billion kilometres is just too far for me to feel the violence of your loss, I'm sorry. I'll imagine the moons instead, peeking over Saturn's rings like silent neighbours watching helplessly as you begin to tremble, burn and break apart.

Sermon (for the burial of Cassini)

Noble Macrocosm; Bespangled Infinity; Great Current illuminating absence with ice. By the force of your data you stilled the chaos of the methane seas, you made the early waters of the flood boil off and cloud over and you composed the tempest over the hexagon of Saturn. As we commit these earthly scraps of our sister, Cassini, to the deepest-deep, grant her retirement and a quick and heavy fire so that she may not taint fledgling life with her fuel. May she cease communication and reside indefinitely as a part of Saturn's complex clouds. Little gatherer of science, indifferent photographer of the dark sublime; we aspire to remember her until that day when all who swallow the air will be embossed with the bald heat of death, which was promised in the future of our sun. We open our mouths in light of what we know, in faith of the evidential and the theoretical, as close to truth as we can muster, for our wonderstruck hearts watching our sweet machine go; Cassini, goodbye.

I fall asleep watching a documentary about Stonehenge, come on my period and bleed through my favourite trousers

I've only seen it through the car window, which – grimy,
squarish – might as well have been the TV.
I could have been lugging huge stones from Wales.

I might have been one of these women – barefoot,
dancing to pipe music. Or the piper (unseen).
Or the cameraman (always unseen) who takes
a moment to focus on the dancer's anklet,

before panning over to the famous stones.
I would've liked to have been this guy – cleaning
fragments of bone with a tiny brush. I'm lugging

the laundry basket downstairs like a martyr. It's not
unerotic to think of your fragments held tenderly
between the thumb and forefinger of an archeologist.

Perhaps I'll give myself a shallow burial in the garden.
Leave a note and a pastry brush. I'd like for you to raise
enormous stones in my honour knowing I wouldn't
do the same for you. The washing machine below

chants *hurry. hurry. hurry.* The sun casts a long shadow
of a leaf across the small painting of a house.
The voiceover repeats the word *Sarsen*

in a low voice until I drift off again. It's not unerotic.

Sestina for Caroline Bergvall

I stood in front of an installation by Caroline Bergvall.
I was struck, not only by the text but by her voice
which had the clarity of running water but also an edge
of music – romance, like someone throwing a rose over their
shoulder, to no one in particular & without looking back.
Heading home, I resisted that bittersweet bus sleep.

Once nestled between three free hours though, I did sleep
& dreamed my house was grand & Caroline Bergvall
came for tea. Having never seen her, it was just the back
of her head . . . the back of *a* head. But I knew her voice.
She pointed to a balcony with no balustrade. *There.*
In dreams I'm always heading towards an edge –

a cliff, a smashed plate, a kerb – though this edge
could be, and probably is, just the end of sleep.
The more I scrubbed the teacups, the more grime there
was inside. I was worried that Caroline Bergvall
was bored but when I apologised for the delay, her voice
came out of my mouth. And then . . . I was back

on the bus, the warmth of the engine – the backs
of many heads ahead of me. Driving towards an edge.
I felt it. I wondered which head contained her voice.
Why a bus? I asked no one. *Is it a metaphor for sleep?*
Driven by the subconscious until we reach our stop. Bergvall
was silent, or maybe she wasn't there.

Then, looking at the rows of heads – an epiphany – *they're all Caroline Bergvall!* Caroline Bergvall with the pink back-pack, Caroline Bergvall with the centre parting, Bergvall with the tonsure & cane, little Bergvall on the edge of her seat naming things, Bergvall asleep surrounded by shopping bags, Bergvall hearing voices.

The bus hurtled on, listing the stops in Bergvall's voice & I feared the destination less – we were all headed there together. If language can be disrupted by sleep, then what is a word but the vehicle we drive back & forth – letters, texts, emails we leave behind, the edge of who we are; the back of a head – never the full Bergvall.

Asleep, I throw my voice over my shoulder. *Bless us! Every Bergvall, here, there & on the bus. & bless these inadequate words, thrown back, as we step off the edge.*

Fleet Services (northbound)

Dawn. I eat a packaged sandwich in a parked car opposite a truck with one man eating a packaged sandwich. Not even one note of certain colour. His eyes chewing the distance. There are moments you can take or not take and I took. In the queue at Shell . . . Texaco . . . I don't know, I thought how beautiful all this would feel later. I know you want the grubby details – you want my dead eyes fixed on that one extraneous scots pine, waiting for an ending. You want my streetlamp-lit lonely euphoria, the bright unkind service-station bathroom, bleach-soaked, pine-effect, 3 a.m. sound of the hand-dryer and my tired eyes meeting the tired eyes of a mother, not mine, in the mirror, and feeling cared for. Well, I have news for you – not everything breaks my heart. And unlike the scots pine, an insomniac surely, unlike the broken picnic table and its used tissues and sex paraphernalia, I continued my drive and that is how I come to find myself not then, the road wrapped around my throat, but here, at home. Snow is falling and I'm toasting my heart, warm with butter. I'm as fertile as a pot-plant and in love. Don't you see? It's you or it's dirt. It's you, even, in the dirt.

I Asked Him to Check the Roof,
Then Took the Ladder Away

All night I enjoyed the lie: *not feeling well, upstairs in bed*
but sends his love. I could feel his frustration

through the ceiling; so strongly that it was as though
my chest were the roof and he was trapped inside.

How will we go on after, I thought, *how will I end this?*

He hadn't called for help. Maybe he'd worked out a way down
but I didn't think so. The dinner party was wonderful.

As the guests left I looked up and realised that there
was no moon. *Shine, darling.* I whispered.

And from behind the chimney rose his little head.

Acknowledgements

I'm grateful to the editors of the following publications in which some of these poems first appeared: *Ambit, Bath Magg, Brittle Star, Lighthouse, London Review of Books, Oxford Magazine, Pleasure Garden, POEM, Poetry Daily, Poetry London, The Rialto, The Scores,* and *Stillpoint Magazine.*

I'd like to thank Back from the Brink, K6 Gallery, The National Trust (Knole House), Royal Holloway University, SPUD (The Observatory), and Tate St Ives for residencies during which I wrote many of the poems in this book.

I'm grateful to Arts Council England, Spread the Word, The Jerwood Foundation, The Arts Foundation and The Arvon Foundation for their support and guidance.

Thank you to my teachers and mentors: Jo Shapcott, Mimi Khalvati, Eva Salzman, Karen McCarthy Woolf, Stuart Silver, Mrs McKay, Jackie, Clive and Guy. A special thank you to Mona Arshi, whose mentorship was vital during the writing of *Passivity, Electricity, Acclivity,* and to Jack Underwood (who edited it for Goldsmiths Press) for all his help.

Thank you to my parents, Naomi and John. To my granny, to Mark and Emily, to Topaz and the brilliant women at Wavelengths Leisure Centre, to Will (trusted reader / sand enthusiast), to Mel who commissioned the Tate St Ives poems, to Ruth, Laura and Tom from Spread the Word, to my agent Claudia Young, to Linder Sterling for this stunning book cover, to my editor Martha Sprackland for her care, attention and belief. Finally, thank you to John Terry (not the footballer) – muse, love of my life, absolute snack.